Burn This Place Down

and Sleep in the Ashes

Artillery Productions

© 2008 by Christopher Cooley

Printed in the United States of America

All rights reserved. No part of this book may be reproduced or transmitted in any form by any means, electronic or mechanical, including photocopying and recording, or by any information storage or retrieval system, without permission in writing from the author or publisher.

Paperback ISBN number: 978-0-9816730-0-4

Library of Congress Catalog Number: 2008902810

Burn This Place Down and Sleep in the Ashes

Christopher Cooley

Artillery Books

A Division of

Artillery Productions

P.O Box 33121

Tulsa, Oklahoma 74153-1121

U. S. A.

For

Jessica, Mairead, Bridie, Ruairi O'Moore

and Nuallain Criostoir Adamson:

That a better world might exist

And for Patricia Cooley:

There are certainly no words

Contents

The First Poem – 1

The New Battle is the Weekday – 2

Malady of the Morning – 4

1:10 A.M. and Broke – 4

Her and I – 5

Now I Can Write Something – 6

It's Too Late – 8

Dead Food – 9

What I did Today was not Good – 9

The American Dream Revisited – 10

Liberating the Organ Donor – 10

Copout of the Year – 11

Patient/Condition – 13

Scum of the Universe – 14

A Midwesterner – 14

Thirty-Five – 15

Hotel I.C.U. – 16

Winter Hymn – 16

Waiting – 17

Poem for Anne Sexton (Wherever You Are) – 17

Suburban Clean – 19

I Will Bleed for the Rest of my Life – 20

To Woman from Man – 21

Washing the Windshield/ The Blood and the Entrails – 23

Friday's Saturdays – 24

The Rabid Dogs – 25

Mother / Father – 26

Exile – 27

My Version of Paris – 29

True Story – 30

A Seasonal Affair – 32

The Times They Aren't A-Changing – 33

She Hangs Dimly – 34

Another Shot at Getting it Right – 35

Mother / Son – 37

Patterns – 38

Books and Telephones – 39

Name the Time, Name the Place (Suicide) – 39

Death; a Mistress – 40

Those Everyday Things – 41

Resonance – 42

Father / Son – 43

Swim Silently Home – 44

Lament for the Late Night – 47

All Poets are Mad – 48

The Hymns – 52

The Insights – 55

Sleep in the Ashes - 57

Preface

Burn This Place Down and Sleep in the Ashes was mostly written in the latter part of 2007. It was one of those times where I saw a repetitive string of occurrences: materialism, death, hopelessness, fear, and loss. There is no strange coincidence that the thematic tonalities of the book intersect almost to a fault. I simply felt the need to make a point about the direction of our world and how I felt about my place in it.

One might suggest that repetition in literature is a dual edged sword: either working for or against you. I would be naïve if I did not recognize that the themes and words enclosed can be found again and again, but I make no apologies for the technique nor do I apologize for the content. It is of my opinion that we as a society have become repetitious and have adopted something akin to what I describe as the "robot ideology".

It is obvious that on every street corner in every city and on every face there is an expression of similarity and it is quickly turning us into one single entity. Originality can still be found, but only long enough for the masses to stranglehold an idea and rapidly reduce it to its lowest common commodity.

I chose a repetitious theme on one hand to perform the mirror image task of hopefully depicting society correctly through my own literal lens. However, I also wanted to experiment with words and ideas to such a degree that maybe people will only understand by way of patterns and repetitive actions. In a certain way, even this you are reading is becoming repetitive.

There is a challenge here then to read between the lines and dig under the primitive skin of what this book has to offer. I am just as guilty as anyone for what I have become, for what this world has become and for the ideologies that hover around us like acrid chimney smoke. There is much to see by the path I have illuminated, but I made very careful steps not to offer any solution other than to start over.

As always, my poems are simply snapshots of what my eyes take in and what my heart pours out. It is, after all, simply the depiction I am after and, unfortunately, I am a man who loves words on paper. If there was another way to put it, I would not bother the scholastic world and its incessant need to scrutinize art and form. Simply stated…this book will not be for everyone.

I do hope that these words have some effect on the reader however, and I trust that whatever might get lost in translation will be made up in the simplistic brutality of the words before you. Putting punctuation in the right place or obtaining collegiate respect never was my aim; getting the average person excited about the power of poetry and what one could do with imagery was.

So there is my apology, my confession, my plea and my fear rolled neat and concise on no more than four pages. I have done what I had to do and now the rest of the burden lies in the hands of you, the reader. Be careful with this book. It cuts cleanly in every direction and it will assuredly fail you at the first hint of disapproval. I was forced to stare at the heart of the world…this is what I saw.

Christopher Cooley

(Winter 2008)

"I will vent my anger in terrifying books. I want to turn the whole human race against me." -- Charles Baudelaire

'Does reality exist? Are we in a real world?' – this is the leitmotiv of our entire present culture. But it merely expresses the fact that we can no longer bear this world, which is so prey to reality, except by way of a radical denial. And this is logical: since the world can no longer be justified in another world, it has to be justified here and now in this one by lending itself force of reality, by purging itself of any illusion." -------- Jean Baudrillard

"It's very hard to reveal yourself. Frankly, anything I say to you is useless and probably more deceiving than revealing. I tell so much truth in my poetry that I'm a fool if I say any more. To really get at the truth of something is the poem, not the poet." ------ Anne Sexton

The First Poem

I belong to the lost generation.

We are the people on the streets,
in the cars and in the dope dens;
on the avenues and in the alleyways;
by the roadblocks and the gasmasks.

We are catatonic cocktail and
religious heretic hay bale.

We smoke gutter leaf stock market razor wire,
chew pesticide laced cupcake debutants,
and practice patricide cash back politics.

Our generation plagiarizes prophecy to
trade wisdom for fornication and profit.
We dumb down intolerance in order to
tolerate, subject subjugation to terms and
conditions we would not expect ourselves
to follow, convict drunks to prison as we,
ourselves get drunk, and betray codes and ethics
to preserve codes and ethics.

We burn nit rice cattle prod shopping mall;
Swallow gasoline fortified with ambisol;.
Manufacture fratricide half-off if buy it now's.

We are hideous halfwit whorehouse and
polluted pixilated photograph.

We are the people in the houses,
in the subways and in the coffee shops;
on the high school girls and football teams,
by the riversides and revolvers.

I belong to the lost generation.

The New Battle is the Weekday

Cars shuttle off by dawn's early light
to dig money out of the ashtrays that are placed beside office building entrances,
to shackle the same slit wrists,
to fill exhausted coffers, in order
to feed pre-washed pocket linings.

Children will be dispensed along neighborhood curbs
in order to receive Leftist, Rightist coffin ships:
Leftist, Rightist education
Leftist, Rightist ideals
Leftist, Rightist politics.

Soup lines come in the form of corporate coffee shops.
Welfare lines come in the form of online garage sales.
Lines and lines of people:
lining up for gas
lining up for lottery tickets
lining up for movies
lining up for gas chambers.

Grocery stores are pastures to feed the human cattle.
Department stores are sweatshops to clothe the human skeleton.
Cell phones are man's best friend.
The dog is a mirror image reflecting ourselves.

Pick up, drop off
Drop in, drop out, drop by
Timepiece, timesheet, time out, times up!
Wristwatch, wall clock, clock radio
Mp3 player, DVD, WMD, PAL, NTSC, IRS.

Image after image depicting shutter speed with
variable rates of perplexity devoured at
meth-like complacency.

The dollar bombers are eclipsing the sun
fertilizing the skies with cocaine powder;

consumerism. The rat has entered the cage
suckling river water from hydro plant
labyrinth racing skin of chrome
necktie noose wearing motherfucker.

The new battle is the weekday.
It comes complete with flack jacket and genocide.
The radio tells you where to go
and the television tells you what to do.
The cost is high and the steaks are center-cuts;
boneless lifeless wisps of ash.

The new battle is the weekday, but only because
the weekend is owned by sports franchise
and outlet store.

So, wage your new war on battlefields unknown,
plant minefields near stoplights,
shine spotlights on mind fields, and tell your
friends what your next plan of attack is:

The new battle is the weekday
The old battle re-released
Version 9.2
Updated just this morning

Malady of the Morning

History holds nothing for man anymore;
it is useless, it is dead and so is my black heart.

We stumble around the city of degradation
fulfilling listless dreams, wiping away childhood memories,
grasping at notions copped from
literature's classical library.

It would be enough, I guess,
to unify oneself with the newest setting sun,
drawing inspiration from the close of the
day knowing that a new one crests the horizon.

But I just cannot.
I cannot look upon the future with anymore hope than the past.
The past has only shown the future
and the future is a tear stained blood red.

If history holds nothing for man
what can the future hold for man?
I say it holds the past
which is only saying
that the future holds nothing.

1:10 A.M. and Broke

It is 1:10 in the morning and I'm broke
I wipe myself off with a paper towel;
reach for the orange juice in the fridge

Tomorrow my daughters will wonder why I am so tired
and my suitcase is half unpacked.
There are too many bills and I am tired of watching T.V.
It is now one-thirty

Her and I

Her and I never had any money,
no we had too many children,
too many dead dreams
too little luck in life.

We were either too Catholic at the time or
daring to risk everything.
I liked to drink or was far too sober
her never giving herself fully to just one thing.

Her and I skirted the issues and made passionate
love less passionate;
nothing there to profit from
never caring about the next month's rent.

We were tired of people,
tired of games,
or simply just tired of living.
We were pathetic capitalists
born out of working-class losers yet,
somehow better off than most.

Her and I were in love,
we just didn't think that
to live
one had to die
in order to put money in the bank.

We were engrossed in just getting by;
just enough petrol to make it just one more mile,
just one more town,
just one more excuse.

Her and I argued little,
no we had too many failures
too many misfortunes
too little luck in life.

We never turned on each other
never sold out for fear
not once passed the responsibility
not once did we let the other person down.

Her and I understood;
by not understanding the world
we actually figured at least one thing out.

We were figuring out each other
we were conditioning ourselves for the last day
calculating the cost of our sins on the
walls of our simplistic estate.

Her and I loved each other
and I guess sometimes when nothing else makes sense
or nothing else happens
than that in and of itself
is enough.

Now I Can Write Something

I could barely take it.

I wanted to write,
to share with the world my visions,
my creations
but the heart quickened and panic ensued
and soon I was engrossed in the mania
that constantly hunted me down.

There were quick successions to make.
First, the Bupropion
followed by Alprazolam
with its chalky remnants littering
the sides of my throat
like swallowing sandpaper.

It would take minutes to kick in;
hours if counting by sundial.
Vision becomes useless
yet society is imaginative
mockery for the god that sleeps above us.
Yes…it would take minutes to kick in
like precious blood sores
untreated, infected, painful.

I will dig in like soldiers do in foxholes across Europe.
I will befriend the grub worm
and take delight knowing others are like me
somewhere in this world.
My weapon I will clean just in case.
I will stay faithful to boot camp
and to my university professors.

Clenched jaw absorbs saliva,
tremors consume hands;
the lunatic universality or the tie that binds us together.

No longer can I taste pharmaceutical flavor,
a worship of hero fades discreetly into closed down strip
malls.

I was brought to this place by bad genetics
or what others might address as shit luck.
To some it was a blessing, to others a curse,
but to me it was just one more child to caress, raise, and send
out into the world.
I was told I would never be cured but assured
I would be made comfortable
which actually made me feel uncomfortable.

But alas, after what seemed like a lifetime of
screaming shrapnel laced silence, the medication
washed over me; a warm wave in an endless sea of
the comfort I was predicted to receive; of the allegiance
I was promised I would get; of the happiness I would
never feel.

The pills were hungry for my organs. Their palates
tailor made for my palates and I resumed my day
as the normal functioning human being; the robot they
wanted; the wounded lion sedate in his cage.

Now I can write something.

It's Too Late

I
have something stuck
in my throat like maybe
too many cigarettes
or
World War II

She wants me to taste her
but I just can't because

I
have something stuck
in my throat like maybe
too many cigarettes
or
World War II

Dead Food

Kill it
Clean it
Cook it
Eat it
Sit on it
Yell at it
Retire it

The American Dinner:
Meat
No exercise
Television
Frustration

Part of a balanced diet

What I did Today was not Good

What I did today was not good. I did nothing today that benefited a soul.

Late at night after many cocktails and delusional undertakings, a man can finally size up his worth and strategically place himself in the order of all human existence.

I calmly place myself at the end of the line and for this I am grateful.

The American Dream Revisited

Four kids
Two dogs
One wife
Debt

The American Dream Revisited
on a cold February night

Liberating the Organ Donor

There was something I wanted to ask you, but
you have already shared secrets with me that
only the dead would know.

I have crawled through this world in my aluminum
cage, pacing the floor like dust mite
and worm. Hollow sensations bewilder my
inner god while petals from flowers fall
through my beleaguered fingertips.

I am ash in urn; footsteps in oceans or the
lone train whistle of downtown America.

Where will you be next Summer? Next Winter?
Will you die again next August? Will we
bury you in mausoleum? I was housed once
in the womb creation gave you. I was fed; breached
by placenta yet that organ has been fed to
a cinerarium I have never met.

The course hands of minimum wage employment
caresses your death, I smoke cigarettes forgetting,
your perfume and mistakes.

We both died that evening. You more than I, yet
nevertheless, we all die a little each day. It is our
homage to life that makes death green with envy.
Death is the step-child; somewhat loved, but forgotten.

In the morning I will wake to another chance at reunion,
even though, like others, I prayed for silent
reconciliation. The subdued whine of a working-class
will forge on without us---we will stay in slumber.

My last words were weak, drowned in humanity
for keepsake. But I meant to say too much knowing thoughts
are like wheat grains that give up before the
harvest. It took so long to have the courage and so
little to not use it.

You are no longer burdened by medicinal nutrition;
you have choked on roast beef for the last time. I will
see you in the haunting, in the stare I have erected as
monument to understanding and until we rise
side-by-side, I will paint sunshine dismal grey and
like water, I will run translucent.

Copout of the Year

They will never understand;
but I was copout of the year.
Maybe it was in the way
I ditched my winter clothes. Or
was it because I threw technology
in the river?
Was it a pose?
A catcall to yesteryear…a fad?
Or was it the way I was fetally
placed , wormwood womb,
peasantry fluid
pure dumb-downed luck?

A copout…yes, me, rebel/heretic/martyr.
Who have I copied? Pessoa? Ginsberg?
I don't read 'HOWL' alone, sipping
coffee in corporate bookstores.
I am not guilty of university tenure,
slick degree colored ivory white with
hints of formaldehyde. The poet's
circle is greasepaint sinister school loan
bourgeoisie bullshit. I should be the
one casting stones, divisive and snobbish.

I have done my homework in halls
of lived experience, real poverty and
no direction. Your Kerouac…your
Baudelaire; a famed future profit unwilling
to fight from beyond cremation.

When did I say I wanted fame and fortune?
It was obvious that I was placed in
alien structure; bone upon bone; flesh
rotting flesh; decrepit weak tenderloin
seared blemished free. A design to
probe the masses of appetites unquenched;
consumerism's bitch
collar wearing monkey dance.

You know what I am saying. Every
breath true, correct, concise, verbiage
homage resplendent, diction from
a glass-keyed Royal Quiet Deluxe.

Copout. Sentimental revival of romantic
documentation (probably false) alluding
to markets unexplored yet still
pulsating relevance
Capital/Kapital --- the line in the sand;
for most the end; a target to aim at or
something in common, because I guess
we now all shit differently. This, no, these

words soon classical literature studied
from afar with no drugs nor alcohol; the
fate of most artists.
Dissecting grammar as if it were actually
important...I don't believe so why should you?
I don't need you to tell me that my poetry
is good/bad. I write for me not you.
I write for weak meaningless people
who can't tell time, can't think, won't think,
don't think.
They will never understand that I was
copout of the year. Will you?

Patient/Condition

condition worsens as doctor releases
me from care. passed around the medical
pale, I am inundated with phone calls
of suspected pimps, but the one I choose
is too busy. condition worsens as patient
waits to see doctor for a full assessment
of what could possibly be another dead
end street. patient is hopeful, will wait
the month and a half, doubtful of being
totally cured and trapped inside a cage
of madness. condition worsens so patient
conforms to the tactics of the brain, lies low
in psychic ditches, careful not to disturb
the sleeping giant. condition worsens
as patient loses sex, appetite, awareness,
depth but gains hardship, inadequacy,
intelligence, self sustaining nature.
condition worsens with all eyes on January
15, the day the doctor is not too busy to
see if condition is worse. patient notes
sand in hourglasses and once again time
holds him stationary in its hand.

Scum of the Universe

We are the scum of the universe
with our Dictaphone mothered in money;
our capitalistic purification centers
hell...nobody is honest here anymore with
what lies we tell our children
each other
every waking second.

So what do we become?
Well...we become the scum of the universe.
We inherit death by sequences, by
scenes, indifferences, incoherencies,
and masturbation.
We enroll ourselves in classes that bear
no witness to truth;
no clarification on what really goes down
black hypocrite and honky white motherfucker

We are scum...half-breed religious fanatics comatose
on laboratory sugar speedballs and
indiscretions and so late in the evening; after
dead food dies in human feast orgy vomit,
we lie silently awake contemplating the
next calendar day only waiting to die
some more;
only waiting to be impaled on dead leaves
and frozen winters

A Midwesterner

I expect to die
maybe someday in the Fall
or maybe by the river near
a desolate Midwestern town.

It might not be by my own hand
but it might, and I imagine a slow
song playing, the catcall of the whippoorwill,
the distant barking of a canine.

Grey stroked sky above, red baked
Earth below, the last images of trees,
water, land. Maybe the thoughts were
blank; possibly they were of loved
ones, regret, denial, fear.

Suddenly or slowly death comes for
everyone and I expect to die maybe
sometime in the Fall
or maybe by the river near
a desolate Midwestern town.

Thirty-Five

Thirty-five years old
Thirty-five years of life
Thirty-five years of betrayal
Thirty-five years of inadequacy
Thirty-five years of breathing
Of walking
Of sleeping
Of denial
Of dreaming
Of restlessness
Of confusion
Of dismay
Of hardship
Of devotion
Of loitering
Of indifference
Thirty-five years old
Soon to be thirty-six

Hotel I.C.U.

I wonder how long the Cross before
me has been hanging there?
It looks slightly to the right; a little
towards the floor and expressionlessly
sad. Someone has painted around it
probably in the last few years. The molding
is grey; a grey that is depressing or shall
I say it has left me depressed.

Heparin, hemoccult, isopropyl, towels,
sharpie: everything in its place.
Half a curtain, many shift changes,
telephones, windowless windows looking
into rooms of the dying. How many people
have died here?

The crucifix has watched them all----
squirming, coughing, struggling to hang
on to anything or anyone. But they were
meant to die since the day they were born and
now is the time to withdraw because
visiting hours are now over.

Winter Hymn

With the onset of winter comes the onset
of sorrow. My soul dies right along with the
leaves. Of who to be in this world
has hidden its face from me. I am forever
lost in the wilderness.
A society built on death and money
is of little interest. But to turn toward the
south is as unbearable as the other direction.

Maybe one day I can stand erect, as sound

as the ocean and as stable as the sun. It is only
in the winter that I die. I will soon have a
new season to plunder. For now I will
waste away in the wind and the rain with the hope
that a gutter catches my fall or a rake finds me
new settlements. With the onset of sorrow
it always will.

Waiting

I am med sick
happy sad
tranquilized despondent
alone tired
hopeful hopeless
bored ashamed
confused hungry
drifting cold.

This morning is another day
to feel human; as human as
possible, as human as I can.
I am delirious
dizzy opaque
worried
but I think most of all I am just
waiting. Waiting for something, maybe
nothing in particular yet waiting nevertheless.
Waiting is hard.
It is all I seem to do.

Poem for Anne Sexton (Wherever You Are)

Anne Sexton, I love you.
I have loved you since the moment we met,
which was scarcely more than an hour ago.
Yes, I admit, I have oft heard your name

spoken in the passages of books great and small
by authors neat and tidy,
looking for validation no matter the consequence
nor time.
Anne Sexton, I love you.
I always have.

Anne Sexton, I love you. But not because
you dared to embrace morbidity and artistic
license, but because I find you haunting and
attractive; the girl I would manipulate for
cigarettes and approval.
Anne Sexton, I love you.
I always have.

To Anne Sexton, whom I adore;
I have loved you this evening, yet I hesitate
to say just why you are here, because some
poor soul pissed on the grave of a mother,
a poet, and a saint. I am neither made of greed
nor lust. I simply host your pose in my
desire and I am nineteen-seventy or
dress size eleven.
Anne Sexton, I love you.
I always have.

To the dearest Anne Sexton, I bid you
farewell. My thoughts as they stray turn to
darker sentiments of flesh residing corpses that
will cajole me into flattering them and not
the book set before me. I offer them a glance at the
beautiful mess that finally has graced me. But they turn
west instead, flippant and defiant, gathering the design
made for television reception and to banish me to
perversion for a girl I can't know.
Anne Sexton, I love you.
I always have.

Suburban Clean

I live in suburban clean.

In suburban clean, everything is
whitewashed familiar; a candescent
light of sterility, the never ending
whine of complacency,
organ grinding dirges to the sheep.

In suburban clean, the wife can ease
the pain with a credit card and babysitter.
She can have her own queer hairdresser and
talk about AIDS, stepfathers and sunglasses.

Suburban clean gives men unearned power,
the subtle homage to the lion where
once he roared free in some distant jungle, now
retires in cages to snack on hydration and
pharmaceuticals. He rinses his mouth with
ethanol breath mints while carnivore
meditation baits his illusion.
No color of skin escapes suburban clean.
We are now simply smarter racists.
The clean cut winter shoes only indefinitely
replace the indigenous summer ones. I
have one pair of shoes to walk through
all of my seasons.

Suburban clean gives the kids a better
education through tutorial diversion
electronically drafted the first of each month.
Various replications meander between
mom and dad; imitation is the best
form of flattery. These little imitating
heathens watch and cavort with siblings
the movement of the hierarchy, aware that
manipulation is the business of the taller gods.
They'll adopt far too many things and the
ferociously tiny, little minds will assuredly misstep

Suburban clean fades human stain so that
everybody is the same and problems become
wrinkled free. Rich people complain almost
more than poor people, their burdens being
greater; their weight harder to lift.
Wine is sport, Sport is life, Life is money, Money
is king. Everybody here dwells in halfway homes,
only staying long enough to find a better
school system.

I live in suburban clean and I have come to
realize that I have never felt so dirty.

I Will Bleed for the Rest of my Life

Days pass through my memory.
I will bleed for the rest of my life.
In extremely short paraphrases
there is a juxtapose that suggests that
we all come to rest in the exact same
place---death.

Going over it in my mind, I see two distinct
images of rot and obsession.
The first image becomes all the more familiar
as distance shortens; the other I am not so sure about.
If I place both frail hands ever so close to the
center of what appears to be the future, I
touch it, but only for a second.

I am positive that loyalty is a forbidden vocation and
a truly alien one to the human being.
We merely seek to devour what lies before us---
a sexual democracy that foretells carnivorous
misgivings wrapped tight in cellophane to be
sold in grocery stores.

The whiskey tastes good tonight. It lingers inside
my mouth much longer than the medication.
I have actually seen the history of misery in my
mind and I will bleed for the rest of my life.
Never mind that all of my passionate crucifixions
will go unnoticed, unheralded.
I can live with anonymity; what I can't live
without is you.

I understand that I will bleed for the rest of my life.
I guess the question is---will you bleed with me?

To Woman from Man

Most women are enslaved to their man,
kept on imaginary leashes and made to obey,
sitting at the foot of their master.

Sure these women act like they are head-of-
the-table. But they are merely hand-out ready;
ready for their wage...a wage they can surely spend
fervently and with the utmost detachment.

Women live longer than men because
they plot to have life where once there was none.
Men have had life by the age of thirty and
therefore do not care what happens except
in regards to money and sex.
His day is over, hers begun but only once
he leaves eggs laid, hatched and bare, seed planted
deep inside the other hens and searching
only for his place to land. Now he becomes
wounded wing and waits to die.

Woman will cry, "I have master not!". But soon,
with silver in hand, she will finally spoil

the kids and make herself look pretty behind
closed doors. Whilst everyone else conjures
adequate memories of the beloved Chief since
passed, her silence will speak volumes
to other widowed corpses and hellish
cackles will soothe the late night martini she
would never have had to drink. She will touch herself
like the many young men of twenty still
rattling around her skull. She conquered
and ravished; they lopping up sour milk and
opiate nectar.

Borrowing phrases from midday conversations,
women throughout the world hold losing
lottery ticket numbers in withered grasps;
never calculating the distance from sun to moon;
never bothering to write memoirs of botched
dinners that were served because he came home
drunk and late and only wanted sympathy and sleep.

No. They will never produce worthwhile
accounts of productivity because the master
never beckoned and only taught them usury
and ill temperament but at least now it is their
obedience and it is obedience well earned.

Tonight, women from shore to shore will
retire with their dreams and desires hidden,
wincing at the pain of their ruler grunting
over them; foul of breath and short of patience.
These ladies are hoping he will tire soon. The
dawn will awaken. The men will shuffle to meet
other kings and finally she can pry herself
loose from the bondage of talk-shows and laundry
and phone calls and department stores can sing
their siren song that emanates…She will hear the
song, blood rushing to the brain, cover the bruised
thighs that laid bear last night and she runs for the door
and she runs and she runs and, unlike the buffalo,
she is free.

Washing the Windshield/ The Blood and the Entrails

Ancient voices inspire us to shed the last little bit
of inhibition that we might have had and secure
for ourselves a place at the master's table.
For far too long the people of this earth have been
steadily walking an unforeseen line headed in the direction
that will ultimately lead to death and destruction.

The breadlines for the poor are long and laborious stabs at
morally righting all for that which is wrong in a morally
bankrupt society. To want to give is admirable. Yet, to then
write it off of your taxes is, at best, questionable.

So, most of us illuminate our lives and work with anecdotes
of importance and charity. All the while, we really only mean
to make money and fleece our neighbors of everything they
are worth. Dignity is foreign, apathy is prolific, the bright red
sun of the morning rises and falls on the fear and lust in
the hearts of men and the optimism of the few still left fighting
for justice and equality are shriveling on the vine and wasting
away. It is comical to watch, a sadness only surpassed by the
hollow stares of the people that pass me by.

I am dead in this place. I was dead from the moment I was
awoken from a slumber intensely personal; in a personal place
with a spiritual person. My anger was passion, but now it is
bitter and soured. My instinct forgotten, I am the animal in the
zoo; the lion who no longer hunts and the eagle that no longer
flies.

Yes I am all of these things now. I am poison in the well.
I am plague and I am nightmare; in a sense I am you.

I understand the rules, I do not like them and I only play
by these rules because I am a coward, I am weak.

At night, in the dark, you can hear the cities asleep, still
restless, nevertheless asleep and succumbing to the recent
nightmare.
He slips out the window, masked and alert, ready for whatever
is asked of him and ever so glad to be there.
If only there were more.
If only there were more.

Friday's Saturdays

It is the end of the line
the end of the song
the end of the story

Life has become the begrudgingly
decrepit example of how the human
has no idea of what to do with himself.
He founders at the crossroads of
existence turned denial mixed with
the episodic idiocy of realization
transformed into comfortable
non-existence.

I will become, for you, depression
unmasked. But you will pay a heavy
toll emotionally for the privilege
of not being able to extol from
the conversation the very meaning of
words you would never understand

In the meantime, you shall pacify
the graces of frontline misogyny
by carefully placing a finger on the
very same neckline that will never
taste esophageal warfare. But for now
it is pleasant just to have her giving
over vaginal fortress and banal
idiosyncrasy; a hog half hollered!

It is ego that benefits these sporadic
humanities I waste on the battlefield of
living a life; it was in my nature
to just roll over and choke on the very
same tongue that would hang me in the
meantime. So what if we finish
out our calendar days
I respond only to the martyr and his
maniacal calculated ways!

The Rabid Dogs

They are like rabid dogs; those
that invade the corporate coffee houses.
It is also in their automobiles that
they spit judgment and venom at passerby's.

These shallow dogs are wide-eyed broken
souls fishing in expensively priced but
cheaply made Third World accessories.
These shallow dogs listlessly pander
to Satan's financial swansong; they robotically
reach for death camp wages and
millisecond mortality.

They are like hogs with the fever:
swallowing decrepit forgotten farmland
bellowing useless factory knowledge
spouting wisdom undeserved;
love unrequited.

They are pawns in a game,
shepherds of gutless flocks,
greedily promiscuous;
hookers of the bank.

But, because they can, the rabid dogs
smell blood on the cloak of humanity,
sense weakness for virtue;

grow insistently tired of those around them.
These rabid dogs are lunatic with disease;
want compassion without granting the same;
void public consensus when
answers are different.

I wonder what the dog sees in the mirror?
I wonder if the reflection lies?
I wonder if Satan kisses gently the mind and
complexion of rabid dog?

They are like rabid dogs, those
that invade the corporate coffee houses.
It is also in their automobiles that
they spit judgment and venom at passerby's.

Mother / Father

Mothers and Fathers pass down acquired
misery to their children; a vain attempt at
vicariously living the life they could never;
giving up on themselves as vindication.

Whether it be failed romance,
wasted education,
bastard renaissance,
shattered dreams,
plate glass resemblance,
Mothers and Fathers hand over thorn
scepter, fool's crown, pathetic dowry.

"Do as I say and not as I do"
"Become what I cannot"
"Inherit the earth"
"Make us proud"

"I gave you life I can take it away"
"You were incubated by state funded
research grants, never mind Mother was

barren, a clear sign from God that we
just should not procreate."

"Never mind Dad was alcoholic!"
"Never mind that you were repeatedly beaten!"

Now go live the life you were given.
Don't ask for money or compassion.
Sympathy is a broken wasteland.
Go pour your old man a drink!

Mothers and Fathers pass down genetic
dysfunction and societal paralysis.
If successful, they will love you all the more.
If a failure, you become…you accept the wrath of scorn
and forget family lineage. The best-case scenario,
or at least the next opportunity, will be grandchildren
who are eternally innocent and the next stage
of indoctrination therapy. Hopefully, somebody
will get it right. The overpopulated earth can
only withstand a certain amount of trauma.
Children will endure but not before the rod
spoils fresh new skin.
It just works out that way I guess…
Father knows best.
Mother knows nothing.

Exile

Youth was a beautiful thing.
Now, looking back on it yet, youth
is faded; as faded as blue jean
or dust jacket.

Life is a young man's game;
a game I never learned to play;
a game with too many rules;
too many consequences;
too many casualties.

Both youth and life are strictly
for the young man. Young men
don't age. No. They do not
flirt with black masses. Nor do they
stare hypnotically at the headstone.

Youth and life are synonymous;
two lovers entwined by canal and
by boardwalk; by needle and shot glass.
They are comrades fighting the same
illustrious opposition---that who is referred
to as Death!

Death! The ancient warrior much
adored and sought after by young estranged
from their parents. They'll sniff
out tombstones in Paris or revel in bistros
where literacy pontificated the era.

Life and Death! Two great Gods---
Baal and Athena.
How readily worshipped these two
astral beings are. How banal they are pursued.
To pursue Life is to pursue Death, whatever
the cost. The youth have little choice, daring
to win a game they neither started nor
can detest.

But! If Life is a young man's game then
so is Death and Death awaits in corridors
long forgotten by Life's lonely agenda.
From the very conception of Life's evil plan,
there has always been options; options
curtailed by twin minds who think in cyclical
unison and control appetites wet with
materialistic servitude.

The twin mind will push, pull at feigned
porcelain veneers, the biblical gnashing;

the equivocal obvious.

This is what drives young men into Life,
into Death! The thing that drives the young, the
youth into the decrepit limbs of Life, of Death, is
that in, being born, the self has only to die
and to prolong, or to expedite is merely to
suggest control which is only to suggest
weakness and fear which is only to suggest
ignorance which is only to suggest
knowledge and the knowledge comes from
existence which for us, as men, merely means
we are nothing more than exiles.

My Version of Paris

I am not here today. No, I
am gone, as gone as the Victrola,
as gone as leprosy.

My mind has cast shadows of
doubt on lands far and wide. But
not today do I break bread with
my beloved Christ, nor do
I temper Satan's hand in the fires of
what I can and cannot have. I will
no longer crave or mourn the
working classes and I will no
longer fidget in beds wrapped
for cancer patients.

I have spat out breast milk, woven hand
over ivory tusk, flittered bohemian
tarot cards at passerby's. No longer
can I taste joy drenched in
name brand perfume. I can sneer at
children focusing, no, training
bewildered eye in directions masterminded
by corporate tongue and wig-wearing old men.

What light can moons cast out of human souls?
Who dares spill blood in ancient kingdom's name?
I am like none of you here. I am swiftly
different in both tonality and verse. This game, this
life you play with tethered wrist and plastic sword, bears
all of the markings of Leviathan and third street.

Please don't ask me to memorize statistics for bread-and-
circus. Oh please do not let me familiarize myself
with Rimbaud or Keats! Mind altering drugs have
their place in town squares, but in my version
of Paris, there sits laudanum before lice.

I am not here today. No, I am
as gone as is yesterday and as here
as is tomorrow's present future.

True Story

This dead place.
This dead art.
Have you no shame for
your existence?
Have you finally done
everything they told
you to do?
Did you go be professors?
Did you do the spoken word?
Did you turn your back on
Ginsberg, Sexton, Bukowski and
Plath because there was no money
in the making?

I was a card carrying member and
I thought you were better. But
little did I know that it
always takes a Christ to uproot

the moneylenders; it always
takes a Judas to keep the weakling
parasites in their place.

You will comb over me when
I am dead and you will cherish
the lice and the grey hairs.
They will become your kingdom
and your source of reflection.
I will be what you wanted. I
always have been what you desired,
but you begged for inclusion and
you sought your entitlement.
Yes. Entitlements are the wave
of the future.
You will give your crown to one,
maybe two, but nevertheless you will
inherit the Earth by whatever means
necessary because you are a bloodsucker
and I have absolutely no time
for weakness because I am strong
and I see the future and the future
lies in the past and I will
commit suicide while you
will commit to memory everything
that you saw, that you could not be,
because yes…you held the key but
for whatever reason you did not
let the lunatic run the asylum.

A Seasonal Affair

In an acutely deformed way,
the wind whipped at my window
by beckoning me outside to play.
I choose to decipher the poets instead.
Unaware of my surroundings and,
though bleak, they are still my
reality, still my amusement.

The sun won't come up today.
No. It will stay under the blanket
of cloud and storm.
It matches my temperament yet
what if the dark could delay
my abuses?
Would I still demand the attention
of the closest of friends and
the stillness of enemies?

How can I save my daughters now?
How can I speak to the splendors of women?
I was mute and I was leprosy;
tangled masses of fear and ego,
disenfranchised,
disemboweled,
mentally cut open and
spiritually gutted clean.

The images that became grafted onto my
skull were as follows:
A gun in hand.
The rape of a young woman.
Cancer.
Stories of the paranormal.
Why do the people choose not to revolt?
Why the two voices in song and verse?

Amidst the chaos of steam and shovel, a
soldier denounces the battles he has waged,

especially those battles in which he was
branded the liar and the slave.
I stand confused whilst all around the suburbs
engines ignite the gas and oil and
proudly ship their masters off to work.

The Times They Aren't A-Changing

So have it your way. I am having it mine;
lest one be the king and one be the slave or
one be the same. We are all now treading
the sick social waters of robot ideology. It
makes perfect sense to want to squeeze
gently on the trigger.

There used to be two games in town:
one game for the one and the second game
for the other. But now they paint horses in
seven mildewed stains that all stink of
normality and sterility; paint brushes dipped
in germ tic, in vodka flavored formaldehyde.

By and large, two separate entities could glean
a thing or two from the other; share, borrow,
produce, and plagiarize with utter disregard for
the lawyers who struggle for the lanyard and cop
feels from the upper-classes. It is myself who must
struggle and it is I who must burden, toil.

The mass populace stares, gaunt are their eyes; a
forecast calling for pain.

They never needed me to remind them of their disaster.
My God, they have the Christ who can never let
them swallow their sin. He knows they will choke, He
knows they will die.

And what about me? Will I die too in the Land?
Will I die in the land of the feudal brave and the

coffers of worthless currency?
Will I ask my son to the table of the whore and pimp?
To the very same table where the feast is the scrap?
To the very same table that crucified the Lord?

I have gone from this place and I smatter the icons
with every ounce of perversion that was heaped
on to me. I foam at the mouth and lick the white
boots of my race. I become detest lest I'm detested and
I feign my most cherished and loving of subjects that
will never know love nor will they ever see redemption. But
it was only my hour and it was only my defenses that
led those to the furnace and led me, the aberration, to the final
alter where I proudly await the whip and I regrettably
receive my pitiful adulation.

She Hangs Dimly

She hangs dimly on the corpses.
But don't we all?
After the summer rains fall, the
water erodes. Instant paranoia sets
in. She wants to be sublime and
she wants to say anything correct.
But the lesson is in the switch;
it beats her until she's blind.

Given the fact that when she bore
two dead sons, the world was
heavy and strapped onto the back of
handsome soldiers. We all must take
a part. We all must take a role. And then,
there are those that just have to take;
they have backseat lines and eat scraps
from the master's table.

Dignified and old enough to know what is

right from wrong, she sanitizes her hands and
forges a new occupation and this will be
her demise---this will be forever…this will be it.

She so desires to be clean.
She so desires to feel justice.
She so desires to exist.
She is so tired.
She is so sad.
She is so clean.

While the ocean floor dusts the dirtiest of
creatures for the noonday meal, a
very successful white male excuses
himself from a table made of very rare
wood; a wood excused by earthly activists
because the price was right, and he gets
up from the table and meets her in an
unattended bathroom.
He slugs her in the mouth.
He pisses on her birth.
He washes his hands without soap.
He, too, is clean.

Another Shot at Getting it Right

Many people have talked about the curse
of their fathers and many have spoke of the
degenerative aspects of family troubles.
I have neither.

My mother, a simpleton, and my father, a monger,
with his books on Hitler and an empty carton of
cigarettes, it is no particular wonder that I am
certainly pleasant and fantastically scarred by any
hope of succeeding whatsoever.

My birth came as a shock and that being said,

it was a Midwestern birth that signified a
perpetually dull existence.
Not marred by my own insecurities or lack of
vision, everyone around me was interested in only
achieving the absolute miniscule of middle of the road.

To top matters off, my friends were the same except for
the odd man out. They felt it his destiny to reach
out and be something that was exposed to be peculiar,
interesting, and above all, exciting. But it wasn't!

Anyway, I had to fill a void, a void left by so
many underachievers. And I got lost and missed the
totality of the exercise and my mission was compromised
and now I had to do something drastic.

The poets were troubled and committed suicide.
The actors were troubled and made too many bad movies.
Alcohol was in everybody.
My choices were slim.
Money?
Revolution? Too normal.
Hell, everybody wanted to be revolutionary.
Department stores carried Black Sabbath tshirts and
shoes with an imprint of Che Guevara.
So let me get this straight:
as I storm Laguna Beach , I can be tracked down by
the F.B.I. because they found my Old Navy Che
Guevara imprint

It was late, the tequila did not take and I had to
go to work so someone else could go play golf.
I couldn't fill the void.
They'd tell me it's my fault.
I should have been more educated or smarter with
my money. I should have been a better thief. I should
have been at the right place at the right time.

I should have waited for my dear old poor cancerous
mother to die. Well I didn't.

I went to bed and I got up and I kissed my girls goodbye
and I went to make money for someone else and
it was all my fault.

Mother / Son

You are the mother.
I am the son.
We both came from one womb;
Rejected
Recycled
Born of the sewer
Rats
Evil.

So many try and touch my mother.
They do not understand her.
She is curious as to why
but still she cradles me in
incestuous stare with cigarette poised.
Sometimes I crave her demands
but alas I have nothing but touch.

It is awful, my days longing
for my mother, but she speaks
to me, only when I can bear to listen,
yes she speaks and tells me to
come home to her and the rest
of our kind.

I love my mother and my
mother loves her son.
I even resemble her in mirrors and
in photographs.
I sexually want her, too and this,
even this
is okay.

Patterns

Sirens wail deep in the city as
the rain begins to blanket
the grass.

I lick my lips and remember
what childhood must have
tasted like knowing on this Earth
that I would never again see the
happiness of youth.

This place has succored my
imagination; a bold attempt at
keeping me alive to carry
out destiny.

Gethsemane is the place to beg for
forgiveness, to ask for another
title only knowing that, in vain,
truth will devour not refrain.

Walk forever trusting simplistic metaphor.

Tonight go by candlelight towards
spacious indignation.

Let the flower of illusion blossom.

Water fields miserably.

Die to live.

Repeat

Books and Telephones

Beside me on the table sits a book and a
telephone. I look to both for an answer;
I look to both for a clue.

The one has not rang and the other sits
unopened. I look at both with a question.
I find something else to do.

Name the Time, Name the Place (Suicide)

Darkness is upon me now. I may never let it go.
Most of us despise the time we were born in. I
despise the time I was born in, yet, useless and worthlessly,
I plod along to the frantic drone of humanities' whimper;
a song for the masses and a requiem for the few.

Life is germinating; I a seed held captive in a jar,
thirsty for water, depraved of the sun, with leeches and
frogs to devour my offspring, multiplying a consumption,
a commodity; a death in full bloom.

Gently I grasp hold of reflections that linger and wait
for the children to tap at my translucent
appendage, my nakedness turned trivial as if existence
was worth absolutely nothing.

Carnivorous young heathens will lap up the crumbs
that were left by past generations, thankful for a taste of
the bloodletting long gone.
We used to hold graves and we could even balance
solar systems. We had alchemy and we surveyed each
other with barbarity. We ate babies for gods to be
loyal and smeared earthen dwellings with history.

I now know this darkness. This darkness is my freedom
and they do not want me freed.

I can now chase the hellhounds. I can now transcend
dimensions. I can build what no empire can hold. I
can bleed when I want. I can die in my time.

Darkness is upon me. It calls me by name. It lusts after
my thoughts. This darkness knows no constitution, but
it does command attention. It will teach me discipline.

If only the older generations would become what is
their destiny, they too, could admit defeat and stand
in the face of the cannon, at the mouth of the river,
at the base of the canyon, in the time and in the place,
and pick their defenses; offer the world only solutions
to what could never be solved. I declare name a time and
name a place and let humanity win no more.

Darkness came upon me and the darkness, well, the darkness,
yes the darkness, well, the darkness it won.

Death; a Mistress

Cannot one recall that death
lurks behind every doorway,
every thought?

The winter brings much sadness.
Yes. My childhood heart is bludgeoned.
It was death that favored me, death:
that beautiful dirge
the omnipotent warrior
the unmoved mover.

Can I not parade around the
dining room table as if some pagan
festival has entranced my spiritual weakness?

Can a man ever be satisfied by his
loneliest song?

Must I smile when the children
rehearse their A, B, C's?

Must I love this world like
rich old people love their money?

Please, dearest friends, leave me
to my mistress and let us send roses
to each other or procure motel rooms to
defile those carnal lusts that are
maritally forbidden.

I do not ask for much. So lend me
this moment to suspend in bleak
gratitude for my doom calls for
me even as I speak.

Those Everyday Things

Things around here are frozen;
petrified strips of nothingness.

I long for what used to be but
they dare not show their faces;
they dare not duel with my fragile emotions.

I was older then…an old soul intent on
doing what old souls do:
lie around
revolution
splitting logs
the occasional trip across the Atlantic.

Women in their corsets.
Men in their bowlers.
Children in knickers.
Dogs, cats, horse and carriage.

Society sat around the fire and
cooked whilst chatting about war.

Slaves were still colored.
Second-class citizens were...well...
second-class.
All was in its right place and order.

Now---we are all the same pathetic creatures,
all of us devoid of moisture and piety.
Every single one of us a liar.
Every single one of us a cheat.

Things around here are frozen;
dead, disgusting and tired.
I wish for the advent of destruction.
I hope for the nuclear winter.

Maybe, in the not too distant present,
I can firmly plant my boot heel on
exactly the place of man immortal and
if this should come to pass I will crush
under heel those that deserve to squalor
in indifference and in all things lukewarm.

These things must happen.
These things must come to pass.

Resonance

Pursued, we are hunted by past
civilizations; present situations.

The low numbing sensation
reflects anonymity in
everything I see.
Merciless assassins have
caught up to me, relentlessly

betraying the Geneva Convention and
the Natural Law.

Although parasitic legions
storm the Vatican, estranged parents
parade children from house to house
to collect modern marvels condensed
by plastic---I have always changed my mind
with cigarette burns and an unhealthy diet.

Later, the television will
speak to lampshades;
the dog will lick Baudelaire's spine.
If nothing else changes and the Earth resists
prophecy, I will still be here, the
reduction of my parents,
the legacy of my offspring.

Father / Son

This waste of terrain with all of
its emotionless banditry, its
white trash bitches.
The city is a whore, all snarled
teeth and perfume and she is
choking on my manhood; my
bile and my buffoonery.

What did I do to deserve this?
Me, a humble man from the place
one easily forgets, I do not remember
the smell of my cradle, but I do
remember my son's and the daughters
that came before him.

Yes my son whom the world will
want to devour, choking him in
faggotry and filth; sickness and credit cards.
All men will bow and quickly

proceed to gnash and wail at his breast.
You cannot wait to get hold of him;
the maniacal plots are already hatched
and with adulation you will reduce him to ash.

Cold, shiftless wars will romance him
in song and story.
Hate will prostultise at the alter where
one day women will rest, entranced by
his sex, all void of dominion over
stark Sunday school; small water large
soft drink.

My son's crowning achievement, the phone
call I will one day receive,
"Dad, I got the job!" he will say,
some wrinkled white-headed vulture
craving pink flesh; baton passing sin's wage tax
"Dad, I got the job!"
"I am proud of you, son"
my knee hitting spit shine pine,
my eye piercing heaven for the grace
any seldom get, I'd hang up the phone,
tell his mother the news, and sob quietly on
the west side of the house.

Swim Silently Home

the mundane
the mutilated
the despised
those in fear
and the lifeless all
gather here to meet me---
the king of misery
with the throne of thorns
adept at holding court
at passing judgment
handing out punishment

absolving sins

hollow sockets dissect
with bleary receptacle
forlorn cadavers
receiving transmissions
from the societal base station
foxhole resplendent
martyr's mythology
school yard bully graduate
parasitical feeder

i never became the host
instead i chose spirit
to walk me up the block
by leash and collar
the vermin scoured the sewer
aroused in their senses
by vomit and failure
they found me
i was sitting there
waiting for blood sucking leech
old man conversation
they found me
the bastard sons
the whore's little girl
the human perception
perfection in third world sackcloth
the disease
the abstention

the exit was nailed closed
by pine-box
by credit
escape route discovered
occupational lockdown
indentured servant reborn
zombie risen
Easter morning redemption
generational fratricide

refurbished casket

i was patient
the pugilist
bobbing and weaving
grasping for ropes
yearning for the bell

the warlords of county apathy
closed in on my cell
dropped nuclear verbal warheads
decimated village and forest
incinerated hut structure
petrol bomb, Bowie knife, Peacemaker
spear
in Babylonian language
confused
arguments ensued
captive/captor
banging drum
pulling rank
Brutus ambition
Caesar's destiny

i manicured my position
filing, shaping
choosing a factory red
apple blossom gloss
the weakness grew tired
sympathetic lustful
admiration for what is beautiful
gnashing teeth horny
i bowed in the shoes
of the chambermaid
blouse torn open
hip socket stretched
labrum crushed
turn by turn
lines lengthened
then shortened

size contorted
breath indifferent
strenuous athlete
failure present
i let them all suck
fetus then formaldehyde
souls became mine
i devoured God's mistake
tore flesh from bone
snorted blood in lines cocained
lapped milk from mother's breast
before puking up nursery rhyme
sunsets fold days into
garage sale veneers
retire worn boot strap
tell dog to bring paper
i worm my way vertical
taste blood
swallow infection
accept nothing
remember everything
go nowhere
leave immediately
lastly
just like firstly
saddle metallic carriage
swim silently home

Lament for the Late Night

I can see hell on my trail.
Whether by cast-call or by moonlight,
I can see hell on my trail.

The whiskey was fine. But those that
support me are demons and frauds. They
choose to persuade me to some other den,
but I will not be forgotten.

I am the lash and whip, the disintegrated
genius born of another. Yet, for now,
I will choose because I want the company
of hyenas, the desert of fools.

I will grace this Earth with the knowledge
of false idols and make sense of perversion
because I am not spoiled with treasures
of the forlorn heart.

They will pick at the breast of stupidity. But
I will raise the bar because they are weak in
their sacrilege; they hunt for new festivity.

It is so easy a child could do it.
I remember their weakness and I am a child, too.
I will go to my maker confused.
I am honesty.
I was never made for this world.

All Poets are Mad

I

Mutations of madness,
all at my disposal
the various weapons that
linger like prostitutes on street corners
there is no discernment
yet rationale now flees in retreat
the heart slightly flutters
the senses are quickened with a
sobering temperament
the body is alive in
electromagnetic shock; an

ocean of despair that culminates
in a sea of tranquility
that few breaths have swallowed
puncturing vessels with waves
of contrived reality

Anticipating nothing except
everything and all
moments like this recede in eternity
at last to retain but a brief
instance of purity
then it is over
it will take decades or more
for this soul to find peace
to be silent and still
be it books or be it living
this life has succumbed to
a restless beginning
a longing or even
a misunderstanding
the voices said
go and follow the muse
They said loiter indefinitely
in sackcloth and ash
conquer the counties
that make up the island
these voices have misled me
with senseless direction
broken compass of
unbearable circumstances

how long until one finds home
when does my madness exist no more
the division between want verses need
is a blind division yet
the darkness of my labors runs afoul
of relativity in the land of
the sheepishly inept
the stranger the sojourner

Certainly in the wrong place
it is for those that are weak
that I sing my song
we may never stand together
never eye to eye
my sacrifice is my mission
my scar is my reminder
of why there is birth
of why we have Christ
there is never an existence
this is all merely circumstance
complete with inherited traits
despite our steel studded grace
we have closed off the levees
forsaken the possibilities
resigned in this life to lose our embrace

II

A somber moment spreads shrapnel
dust clouds drain sympathy from
normally nice folks
there dare not be one single breath drawn
because clocks tick sequentially like
baby breaths, never choking entirely
on what once was an object of lust and of
old men's hands, now a test tube secreting
protein; manna for the exiled
What went wrong in the Garden of the Lucky?
Would I, too, have eternally fucked up?
Does it matter?
Two men speak, engorged in treaties and
dull subtle nuances
Men are bound by currency, commonalities
to relate so fear can subside

But man beats his chest and bangs his drum
only to cower; bend at the knee of a flashy
car or a beautiful girl

Stalin fell, Samson diminished, the First Bank
of American Greed toppled and reduced to
whoring in the streets, do I dare speak contempt
for Capital?
Must I pledge my allegiance to the greenest of flags?
Windows, the human equivalent to the fishbowl,
show theatre misery and the weather
I would never know sterility, not even in the
white washed sick houses of which I was born but
now I scrub these hands tremendously well making
sure no diseases stick; diseases I crave but only to infect
and make my transformations complete

I look to the sky, the sun, disjointed of happiness
a heart plunged deeper into despair like
river rocks helpless to the power of the tide
half the man, half the human, nourished by
scientific experiment, devoid of feeling
the unattended play in the third act
even this, the swansong that separates me
from them, is no longer manageable
it is early in the morning that I feign at
the twilight of a life, of having a chance at
something other than what is put before me
I could be anything in this world, but to be
anything would take everything and I am
bankrupt of everything
there is nowhere for this soul to weep;
no corner hides the face of one who won't replete

I need a place to retire
to spend my days in bathrobe and hypnosis
a place to smoke my pipe and spout gibberish
to the nobody that is around me
somewhere I can impale society's whim
a new home to defile
the best place to derail my psychosis
the hollowed burial ground of my ancestor's voices
anywhere but in the present tense
a sweeping epic in grandiose proportions where

finely manicured lawns await me
in the manor of a madman because you see
all poets are mad and if you really don't believe me
just start again at the top of this poem
and all will be revealed in due time
I promise

The Hymns

Hymn One

I want nothing from this world.
Nothing this world has to offer is for me.

Man stares fanatically into the mirror;
piercing eyes panicking;
entertaining demonic thoughts;
greed whore scum.

By despotic holler, factories grind
out alms in sacrificial weather.
I shudder inside wishing my children to
grow quickly, passing this world by.

Hymn Two

Is the best one can do nothing?
Is it fair to react symbolically?
Do I dare haunt my hope?

I tied my hands behind my back and threw
myself overboard to see if I could swim and
not drown. I refused to loosen the ties that bind
me and I do this forever without recognition.

Hymn Three

Until we remember to forget, we
will forget nothing and remember everything.

The comedy of life is that we take ourselves
to be honestly real, never knowing that our
reality was simply illusion as truth.

Hymn Four

Whenever the voice speaks,
that tiny little voice somewhere
deep inside of your soul,
whenever that voice speaks,
you should listen intently.

It will be the only good
advice you will ever receive.

Hymn Five

People are a source of frustration.
They carry dead weight on their back.

Why do we roam in herds of death with
no ritual? Why do we conform to no rule
of thumb?

Maybe we are just a canvas to paint and the
picture is simply beside the point.

Hymn Six

Nothing I do makes sense; it only
makes more nonsense.

I try and pin a response on my actions in
the daylight, but at night I tremble in
ignorance and disbelief.

Hymn Seven

Fear is weakness realized.
There is nothing to fear.
Fear fears nothing.

I was young and afraid.
I am now old and fear nothing.
What is there to fear except
maybe fear which is not realized.

Fear fear when fear is near.
Don't fear fear when it never appears.

Hymn Eight

Faith has no dominion over me---
It is simply bothersome, quaint, ugly.

And the world is tricky. It places leaves
over your eyes to see only rot and grub worm.

So I plagiarize all of my days;
a steady hand to betray morality once again;
I want nothing from this place.

To stand guard over tradition is pointless.
We are too old to quarrel with spirits.

In my nightmare sleep, I recoil like the extinct
African snake; hissing, moaning, flesh-rotting
heartache, yet, still breathing.

I have come to the place of nonsense and
I now expect myself to make sense of it.

This is what plagues and beleaguers me.
This and only this.

The Insights

1.

I guess it was so important to want to become something. I would be anything, yet I wanted to really be nothing and just let nothing be exactly what I was. In being nothing, I really became something, and now that I am something, I really understand what it means to be nothing.

2.

It was a desperate need to feel the hand of originality across my back. I am ashamed in my skin and I crawl towards the darkest plain of non-existence. Everybody here holds title except for me. I am strange. Alien. Vaguely aware of what the world does to a man. I profit now like dogs and tear at rotting flesh or scraps from the table. It was never my intention to become so unlike the other people here. It just happened.

3.

My stomach is growing tired of food and my mind is growing tired of images. All day long I cram steaks into my belly and visions into my brain. Late at night, I pacify my incessant need to be immortal, all the while, hating almost everyone around me. So why do I want to be remembered by those I dislike? Good question.

4.

Morality and ethics---they weave a web of deceit inside of my soul so I neither know which is good and which is bad. The enemy to me is that of the self, or maybe it is the person standing before me. I should get out before it gets too late and then I cannot undo what it took so long to destroy in the first place.

5.

Title! It is so important to the narcissistic side of my ego and conclusion, although bereft, haunts me down every single hall in this house. It is way past the point of doing right or doing wrong. I am now at the point of delusion and fear and I reach out for somebody else's history all day long. I could have made a thousand myths by now, but I wanted to immolate and instead I imitate. The line is no finer than that of the table before me.

6.

I have the hands of the working class, the mind of the mystic, the heart of the apostle and the motions of the thief. It is easy to see why I am so confused.

7.

Why does it seem so easy and yet I know that it always has to be hard. The long road, the short-road, the middle-road---they are all just roads and the walk is the same in any season, for after all the walk is simply just a walk.

8.

Praise is elusive. Money comes and goes. I hang on to praise as if I were to never spend the very dollar I earned. I would be loved but hungry.

9.

I am tired of trying to figure out what it means to become something important or successful. Why should I care if anybody cares and why should I want to be adored by those I do not care to be with. I figure I have filled my ship with souls and I should just make do with whatever they adorn me with.

10.

Maybe somebody will one day discover the man that I am and they will tell me how important I am and they will lavish me with gifts and they will hold me in high esteem and I will believe them.

Sleep in the Ashes

Burn this place down and sleep in the ashes.
This is what I say!

Everything around me is dead:
building and concrete
humanity and feeling.

The train rolls beside me, but
from on my perch I shall not be
bothered by contraptions of yesteryear.

The sun will soon set, the moon will
take hold, the wind will blow silhouettes
right past my mortality.
It was on these bricks, maybe eighty years ago,
that young men prospered or dreamed of better days.

Now, with the stockyards closed and the beggars
being king, I wish for the rain to wash this filth and
for God to send ships so the sailors can survive.

This world needs to end because beauty is scarred;
love is commodity.

Send us the fire; the match to strike fields to
their knees; animals to their maker.
Burn this place down, level the horizon, cut wrist,
bone, and tendon; knock unconscious evil brain---
the impure heart will stop.

I tasted fear but once, not in relationship, nor commerce,
but once in myself, I found favor in untruth, in hiding.
Now that we hang ourselves by mistrusted threads and
alcoholic vines, my trusty spiritual knife has frayed the
bonds of physical presence and I fall through the cosmos
awaiting an impact, predicting an end.

Burn this place down and sleep in the ashes.
Cover the beds in animal skin and hair shirt.
Crawl to the grave. Erect the best headstone. Make
friends with the worm. Make love to the soil.

The death men seek is able and willing.
It is pure.
It is just birthright and destiny.
So burn this place down. Take back the heavens.
Give back some money and sleep in the ashes.

"I bowed out of life before it began, for not even in dreams did I find it attractive. Dreams themselves wearied me, and this brought me a false, external sensation, as of having come to the end of an infinite road. I overflowed from myself to end up I don't know where, and that's where I've uselessly stagnated. I'm something that used to be. I'm never where I feel I am, and if I seek myself, I don't know who's seeking me. My boredom with everything has numbed me. I feel banished from my soul.

I observe myself. I'm my own spectator. My sensations pass, like external things, before I don't know what gaze of mine. I bore myself no matter what I do. All things, down to their roots in mystery, have the colour of my boredom.

The flowers Time gave me were already wilted. The only thing I can do is pluck their petals slowly. And this is so fraught with old age!

The slightest action weighs on me like a heroic deed. The mere idea of a gesture wearies me, as if it were something I actually thought of doing.

I aspire to nothing. Life hurts me. I'm not well where I am nor anywhere else I can think of being.

What would be ideal is to have no more action than the false action of a fountain – to go up so as to fall down in the same place, pointlessly shimmering in the sun and making sound in the silence of the night so that whoever dreams would think of rivers in his dreams and smile forgetfully."

--- Fernando Pessoa

The Book of Disquiet

Christopher Cooley is the author of two books. He has written hundreds of songs, several articles, essays, and is currently scripting and producing two documentaries. He lives in Oklahoma with his wife and four children.

Artillery Productions, LLC was founded by Christopher Cooley and produces poetry, spoken word, music, nonfiction, and documentary film. For more information please contact:

christopher@christophercooley.com

or write:

Artillery Productions

P.O. Box 33121

Tulsa, Oklahoma 74153-1121

United States of America

Special thanks: Everett Estes, David Wagoner, C.L., Devin Cooley, Mike and Andie, Warren Stewart, and Brian Pryor. As always to Jessica for listening. To Anne Sexton for the vision and Charles Baudelaire for the reason. The rest know who you are…

Poetry will come back when all is said and done. You just watch! When the lights go out and the electricity fails, the omnipresent fact of words is irrefutable. Have your television and computers…in the end the typewriter and the voice will still be the viable sources of communication. Let's hope they still make ribbons and conversation. If not, our doom is certain.